LONG-DISTANCE RELATIONSHIPS

Amazing Secrets, Communication Tips and Relationship Advice For a Healthy Long-distance Relationship

Carrie Butler

TABLE OF CONTENTS

Conclusion

INTRODUCTION

Perhaps you've just started seeing someone great after endless searching and you both get along, have some good time together, and things appear to be working out perfectly. The only problem? They got a job proposal in another state or on the other hand, perhaps you hit it off with someone cool online who ends up living on the opposite side of the country. No matter how much you love each other, there's probably a part of you that wonders how or if your relationship will survive the long distance between you.

First of all, be comforted in knowing that long distance relationships can absolutely succeed. In fact, most couples find themselves separated by miles and miles of distance at some point during their dating or marriage relationship. Many couples even point to a season of long distance as the cornerstone of a stronger relationship. However it could appear to be scary or testing at first but, a long-distance relationship can succeed — and they do all the time. They simply require a touch of additional effort and consideration.

CHAPTER ONE

AMAZING SECRETS TO MAKE YOUR LONG-DISTANCE RELATIONSHIP WORK

In a bid to answer frequently asked questions by lovers (Young adults and even married couples) in Long-distance Relationships (LDRs), here are a few amazing secrets to keep your hopes alive, even from a distance. Questions on how to keep the love anew and tackle potential issues that could come up will be answered.

Local and long- distance relationships require a great deal of exactly the same thing for optimal relationship health. Long-distance ones, notwithstanding, will require somewhat more cognizant thought. Individuals in long-distance relationships should be much more purposeful and productive in accomplishing the work that assists relationships with flourishing.

Maintain your Independence

It's okay to feel like a piece of you is missing if your partner is miles away, but try to keep up with your usual routines. Keep in mind, you're not simply a part of a unit — you're as yet your own person. It may likely interest you to know that keeping occupied often helps relieve feelings of loneliness. If you don't see your partner often, you should chat with them all the more habitually. Be that as it may, feeling attached to your telephone or PC can prompt trouble, or even hatred, that is if they can't necessarily converse with you. You'll likewise miss out on important schedule with other friends and family.

Regardless of whether you have the opportunity and energy to talk continually over the course of the day, it's as yet really smart to invest some time all alone or with loved ones.

Be there, even when you can't actually be there

Adhere to your 'meeting' times whenever the situation allows. You would have no desire to date somebody who continues to miss in-person dates for very long, would you? Actual distance can here and there cause a relationship to appear to be more casual. In any case, focusing on your partner, similarly as you would while dating somebody locally, is critical in making long-term relationship work.

A partner who's excessively far away to assist when things turn out badly may stress more than a nearby partner when they don't hear from you at a normal time. Obviously, things will come up, but try to tell your partner at the earliest opportunity. Also, if you can, plan a make up talk chat session.

Try not to disregard sexual intimacy

Keeping up with sexual intimacy is a vital test in some long-distance relationships. Assuming you and your partner appreciate ordinary sex, you could battle with the absence of private contact during your weeks or even months apart. But you can in any case associate intimately, even from a distance.

Few tips to attempt to keep intimacy intact. Try:

- *Swapping attractive photos (Always ensure your Messaging app is secure)*

- *Discussing sex and things you might want to attempt*

- *Sending sexual messages or letters*

Simply remember not every person feels cool with digital intimacy, so consistently examine and set individual boundaries around photographs, telephone sex, or webcam use. It's normal to feel a little shy at first, but don't hesitate to bring up these feelings. After all, sharing awkward moments can often help you build more intimacy.

Share physical reminders of each other

Your loved one's belonging can convey a great deal of

importance. Consider their toothbrush in the restroom, their number one jam in the cooler, or even the aroma of their cleanser on the bed cushions. These can all assist you with recalling your partner's presence in any event, even when they're many miles away.

  During your following visits, consider deliberately leaving a few possessions with one another. Hang up some garments in the storeroom, leave books on the rack, and purchase a most loved brand of tea or espresso to abandon. The following time you visit, those things will be waiting. Furthermore, at the meantime, they could help both of you feel like the time until your following visit isn't quite long as it appears.

Hang out at any possible chance

  Time, money, and work responsibilities can all make it hard to visit your partner frequently as you'd like. Think about doing a timely arrangement to get a fair setup on transportation or investigate elective transportation choices, for example, trains or boat rides.

Having shared experiences with your long-distance partner increases the cohesion of your relationship. Finding things you can do together also pays off big time in helping you feel more connected. That's a huge win when it feels like the distance is pulling you in two different directions. You could try switching things around by meeting at a midpoint to ease up the burden (and explore a new city all together).

More things to try:

Strolling through the grocery store, you hear a couple discussing whether to make burritos or risotto for dinner. You feel an ache of jealousy that you don't get to shop with your partner. However, actual distance doesn't mean you can't do things together, particularly with current innovation. It simply requires somewhat more imagination.

Watch a film together

On account of the ascent of streaming, you can watch films or TV programs on opposite sides of the world. Synchronize the start of the film by beginning at the very same time. One partner could likewise watch through webcam while the other partner plays the film, however this can make it harder to see or hear (Though this may not make any difference if you're watching "Good fellas" for the hundredth time). Partake in the film with your partner by calling or video chatting while you watch. This method might require some investment to become acclimated to, obviously. Yet, after a short time, you'll presumably wind up similarly as loose as you'd be assuming they were in the same area with you.

Take a walk

Share a stroll with your partner by chatting on the telephone while you invest energy outside in your area, a most loved spot, or some place totally new. You can specify any new or fascinating thing you see and even take pictures, if conceivable, do this while they're going for a walk, as well. Organizing to do a similar action simultaneously can build your feeling of association. Walking and video chatting at the same time may not be the most secure choice, so track down a most loved park or other calm spot to have a brief video call.

Make a go of a hobby together

Hobbies can challenge you, assist you with taking a break in an enjoyable manner and promote relaxation. If you and your partner both have sufficient opportunity to try out a new hobby, consider observing something you can do together.

If you plan to video call or chat on speaker mode, search for hobbies you can do at home. A couple of choices to consider:

- *Sewing*

- *Woodwork*

- *Painting or drawing*

- *Baking*

- *Cooking*

- *Yoga*

- *Learning basic foreign languages*

You could in fact do various things at the same time. Video calling while one of you rehearses guitar and the other sketches for instance, can look like the sort of evening you could have while physically meeting each another.

Cook and eat a dinner together

Assuming you and your partner like to cook together, push the tradition along in any event, when you're apart. Try making a similar dish and check whether they turn out something very similar — Anyways keep your telephone or PC away from any food or fluid!

Plan a night out

Perhaps you can't go out on the town together in person, yet you can in any case make a heartfelt environment at home. Put on music and have a glass of wine (or your number one beverage) together. You can cause the evening to feel more unique if both of you:

- *Spruce up*

- *Light candles*

- *Make a dinner you both appreciate*

- *End on a heartfelt note with a video visit during a candlelit shower and private discussion.*

Remaining associated like this can be particularly significant on the off chance that one partner lives alone in another city with no friends and family close by. Simply ensure that rest of the group realizes they'll have a digital guest.

Do chores together

A great many people don't actually anticipate their errands. Dishes, clothing, cleaning the toilet — these assignments probably aren't your favored method for going through an evening, particularly in the case where you have to do everything all alone. You can't help each other out from a few hundred miles away, yet talking while you work can cause errands to appear to be less tedious.

This most likely won't work with everyone. It's suspicious both of you need to watch the other wiping channels or cleaning out the litter box. However, attempt a clothing closing date or talk while clearing out the fridge (they could even have the memorable option what's in that Tupperware you're hesitant to open).

Know your partner's love language

We all get our needs met differently, some of us need quality time, some of us need compliments. Know your partner's love language and make things work out just fine for you.

CHAPTER TWO

COMMUNICATION TIPS FOR A HEALTHY LONG-DISTANCE RELATIONSHIP

Examine communication needs

Whenever you initially start a long-distance relationship, discuss how frequently you need to talk, beyond quick messages over the course of the day and make sure you both are on the same page about it. You could both agree you need to talk much of the time yet differ about what that really implies. If your ideal levels of communication vary, observing a trade off almost immediately can assist with forestalling disappointment later.

Create a communication schedule

A communication schedule can likewise help. This

schedule doesn't have to stand firm, however you might feel comforted realizing when you'll hear from your partner next. An occasional, unconstrained, "thinking of you" call can be a nice surprise, yet planning longer discussions can assist you connect when you're both at your best. If your partner is an evening person and you're a greater amount of a morning person for instance, take a stab at arranging calls for not long before or soon after dinner.

Some people in relationships especially young adults and couples want to feel connected every hour. Some find it tedious to talk every day. Well it's easy, discuss with each other what works for the general frequency and length of time you will spend texting, talking, or video chatting in a day or week. And be open to modifying your communication tendencies as life creates new and unexpected demands.

Responding to each other's emotional calls can seem tricky within a long distance relationship. You can't physically show up for each other's milestone days or reassure someone with a hug, you know, but that does not make this crucial element of relationship success any less important. Instead, long-distance couples may need to be more intentional about responding to each other's attempts to connect.

If you've scheduled a time to talk with your partner, make that call a priority, just as you would any work meeting or doctor's appointment. If your partner has an important day, call or text to find out how it went. By weaving your partner's needs into your day, you'll demonstrate that you're there for them, no matter how far apart you might be and you'll see that it works great.

Vary your modes of communication

Switching up how you stay in touch might assist you with feeling more connected. You could share photographs and recordings with Snapchat, keep up a talk on Facebook Messenger, message now and again, and settle on a fast telephone conversation over your mid-day break or when you get up in the morning. Well, note that certain individuals get overwhelmed while monitoring multiple discussions, so this may not work for everybody.

You may likely:

- Consider attempting non-digital methods of communication, as well. Receiving a letter or an unexpected package tends to brighten most people's day.

- Try sharing a letter diary or scrapbook brimming with notes, pictures, and tokens from your regular routines. Send it to and fro, alternatively adding to it.

Make the most of your communication

In a long-distance relationship, it's not unexpected to feel like you never get sufficient time to chat with your partner. If this sounds familiar, attempt to zero in your energy on making the most out of your communication. As you consider things to share over the course of the day, write them down so you recall them later. If you have something on your minds, let them out rather than leaving things unsaid. Don't neglect the mundane

Distance can keep you from feeling close to your partner but worse still, lacking minor details can cause you to feel considerably farther apart emotionally. Your sense might lead you to settle for major or significant subjects so you can cause the discussions you do have to count. Yet, little things that don't exactly make any difference at the end of the day likewise add to your image of your partner and further deep emotional connection.

Along these lines, vent or meander aimlessly to one another and don't hesitate for even a moment to share things that appear to be unimportant, or better still, boring — what you had for lunch, your new neighbors, or how you stepped in cat vomit on the bathroom floor. All things considered, you'd presumably tell those things to a partner you saw everyday.

CHAPTER THREE

RELATIONSHIP ADVICE FOR A LASTING AND HEALTHY LONG-DISTANCE RELATIONSHIP

Like any sort of relationship, long-distance relationships are certainly not a one-size-fits-all circumstance. What works for one couple probably won't do much for another. In any case, there are a couple of things you ought to most likely try not to do in that frame of mind of long-distance relationship.

Try to possibly avoid:

Investigating your partner

Long-distance relationships require you trust each other to keep up with the limits of your relationship. Obviously, this goes for each sort of relationship, yet it can have considerably more importance in a relationship where you have no chance of knowing whether your partner is really doing what they say they're doing. It's generally expected to stress when your partner's way of behaving appears to be uncommon. Perhaps they miss a goodnight call, gab about new friends, or appear to be less receptive to texts for a couple of days.

 At the point when this occurs, impart your interests as opposed to allowing stresses to entice you into requesting evidence of where they were or photographs of them in bed every evening.

Dealing with each visit like an excursion

 If you only see your partner periodically, you could want to make the entire visit advantageous. While this is absolutely justifiable, it can make it harder to know what your partner's life resembles when you're not there.

Hushing up about sentiments and feelings

Assuming that you like to discuss troublesome feelings or sentiments face to face, you could battle to track down ways of offering these things to a long-distance partner. In any case, staying away from genuine conversations can ultimately create some issues. Your capacity and ability to discuss troublesome issues or sentiments are both vital. Many individuals will more often than not be avoidant of these things, since they're hesitant to cause feeling or upset.

Furthermore, the shortfall of looks or non-verbal communication can make it simple to misread words or expectations, which can make errors more probable. Notwithstanding these troubles, it's essential to start discussing your sentiments with your partner. Concealing your sentiments, or lying about them, won't help both of you over the long distance.

Trust issues

It may not be practical for you (or your partner) to

promptly answer to messages or calls. In any case, you could see, when you do talk, that they appear to be occupied or unbiased. If this turns into an example, you could feel stressed, even envious assuming you realize they invest a great deal of energy with different companions. If you're the one arranging every one of the visits, starting communication, and sending shock care bundles, you'll probably wind up feeling baffled down the line, also to some degree shaky about your partner's warm gestures. One response to this issue? Better communication on the two sides.

  Assuming that one of you has less enthusiastic energy because of work commitments or stress, discuss it. Having a legit discussion about what you can both sensibly contribute can assist with lifting a portion of the weight and guarantee you both have a real sense of safety.

Advice for your long-distance relationships to work

positively

Long-distance relationships now and then include less struggle normally. Conflicts over tasks or family assignments, for instance, presumably won't come up. However, assuming you truly do have a distinction of assessment, it's vital to say as much, particularly when it includes individual qualities or things that truly matter. Emphatically contradicting perspectives can prompt clash, however they can likewise assist you with perceiving that a relationship may not work out long distance.

Try not to avoid having conversations about serious topics, regardless of whether you accept you could wind up conflicting. Attempting to keep the relationship awesome and struggle free can mask contrary qualities or hold you back from developing as partners.

Here are the tips that can assist you with exploring conflict beneficially:

Respect the reason why you're apart

There's no doubt you'll have days when your long distance relationship seems especially difficult. You might even be tempted to do something impulsive—like quit your job or drop out of school—just so you can be together with the person you love.

While that might sound romantic, remember there's an important reason you're living far away from the person you love right now. That reason may hinge on a professional, financial, or family situation that needs to play out properly until the timing is right for you both to be together geographically.

Don't let months or years of progress go to waste out of impatience to finally be together. Your relationship will be stronger in the long run if you finish what you've started and finish it well.

Create a long term plan for merging your worlds, when the time is right

Anyone who's been in a long distance relationship can attest to the underlying heartache of being apart from the person you love. If you're in a relationship with the person you want to spend your life with, at some point you'll need to craft a plan to join your worlds together.

Whether this involves a wedding, an engagement, a job change or a relocation, be sure your plan considers the right next step at the right time for both people. Having the hope of being together long term can help you ride out the toughest days of being apart from one another. That little bit of hope can go a long way toward making the one you love seem not quite so far away.

CHAPTER FOUR

CONCLUSION

Perhaps you've gone through the book and have taken down tips on how to sustain a healthy relationship even from a distance, do make sure that these step-by-step guide is adhered to for your own relationship to come alive. Remind your partner frequently what you love about your relationship. Doubts, insecurities, and jealousy can run high in long distance relationships simply because you're spending so much time away from each other. This is why therapists recommend using frequent verbal assurances with one another. They help minimize these negative feelings and clarify where you stand as a couple.

The next time you both talk, tell your partner how much you love and appreciate your relationship. And if you're feeling uncertain about where you stand, don't be afraid to ask for reassurance for yourself. A simple "I love you and wish we could be together today," is as wonderful to say as it is to hear. Distance does not have to signal the end of a relationship. Sure, you might have to put in a bit of extra effort and get creative with how you stay in touch, but you might find that those elements just bring you closer together. It doesn't necessarily have to be the case that your long-distance relationship doesn't work out, simply follow these tips and maintain love even when you're 1,000 miles apart.

Long-distance relationships also work!

Printed in Great Britain
by Amazon

81769991R00021